BUTTERFLY BONES

Larry Butler

TWO RAVENS PRESS

Published by Two Ravens Press Ltd
Green Willow Croft
Rhiroy
Lochbroom
Ullapool
Ross-shire IV23 2SF

www.tworavenspress.com

The right of Larry Butler to be identified as author of this work has been asserted by him in accordance with the Copyright, Designs and Patent Act, 1988.
© Larry Butler, 2008.

ISBN: 978-1-906120-24-5

British Library Cataloguing in Publication Data: a CIP record for this book can be obtained from the British Library.

All rights reserved. No part of this publication may be reproduced, stored in a retrieval system, or transmitted in any other form or by any means, electronic, mechanical, photocopying, recording or otherwise without the prior written permission of the publishers. This book may not be lent, hired out, resold or otherwise disposed of by way of trade in any form of binding or cover other than that in which it is published, without the prior consent of the publishers.

Designed and typeset in Sabon by Two Ravens Press.
Cover design by Two Ravens Press.

Printed on Forest Stewardship Council-accredited paper by MPG Biddles Ltd., King's Lynn, Norfolk.

Mixed Sources
Product group from well-managed forests, controlled sources and recycled wood or fiber
www.fsc.org Cert no. TT-COC-002303
FSC © 1996 Forest Stewardship Council

About the Author

Black Sheep in the Family

Me or Uncle CC? Everyone called him CC; his real name was Clarence Cecil Short. I'm blacker because I left America and never came back. CC is less black. After touring the world in the Merchant Navy, he came back. Inherited Grandma Short's house – did it up and sold it, then bought two more houses. Eventually he bought the whole town of South Pekin, Illinois. He was a real estate man, a slum landlord during the Depression. He owned two whore-houses and a herd of rent boys. During his time in the Merchant Navy he collected tattoos all over his body – even his penis – but you could only see the design when it was erect. I won't go into detail. He was buried fifteen years ago with a Swiss bank account number tattooed somewhere on his body – so the rumour goes. My mother employed a detective to try to access the account and get the money. He was probably worth millions.

I started turning black when I failed everything at school. But maybe I'm blacker than CC because I fought for the voting rights of Afro-Americans, civil liberties for Chicanos, better pay for Mexican migrant workers in California, and crosses were burned on my lawn in Bakersfield after I infiltrated the John Birch Society (the western equivalent of the Klu Klux Klan); and because I was convicted of treason and given a five-year prison sentence and a $10,000 fine for helping people desert from the army and finding them safe homes in Europe. I was living in Paris at the time – 1967 – at the height of the Vietnam war. The peace group was based at Shakespeare & Son on the Left Bank, where we printed anti-war flyers and posters. And because I never went to prison and never paid up. Instead, an English woman agreed to marry me which prevented the US government from extraditing me. Because I burned my passport. Because I burned the American flag.

Over a twelve-year period I became really black – or maybe red – in the eyes of the FBI, who visited my parents every six months. And because I've never had a proper job. Because I've been divorced twice. And blacker now because I'm living with a German woman with a Sanskrit name (or is it Pali?) and have a British passport.

But when we visited Uncle CC in South Pekin in 1949, he took me and my sister (she's the white sheep, a certified public accountant) to a big department store like Macy's, and he said "Ya can have anything ya want." He was my hero then, and my horse when I was geared up in my Roy Rogers cowboy suit, hat and spurs – the very suit I wore when I started thieving at Dick's Supermarket on the corner of 4th and Orchard in San Jose. I never got caught, but I slowly turned black from inside out.

Acknowledgements

I would like to thank my readers who have offered me support as well as challenging criticism – particularly Gerry Loose, Tom Leonard, Linda Chase and Linda France; the Scottish Arts Council for a bursary in 2006 which gave me time to put this collection together; and David & Sharon at Two Ravens Press for accepting it for publication.

Some of these poems have been published in magazines and anthologies, including *Island, Poetry Scotland, Sweet Sour & Serious (Survivors' Press), PlaySpace, The Heart of Origami, Needs Be, Painted Spoken, Essence.*

Contents

After the bones

After the bones	3
that sounds like the beginning of a poem	4
Butterfly Bones	5
Goodnight Kisses	6
Hindrance	8
stale memory	10
Mother Crosswords	11
negative capability	12
Frogs at the Funeral	14
The phlebotomist	17
Lines on the River	18
Real revolutionaries stay at home	20
Baking Bread	22
the anger will endure in language strict and pure	24
Crinan	25
The neighbour's telly's too loud.	26
57 All Saints Road	27
Upper Ostaig House	28
constipated in the USA	30
Bones	31
Forty Years On	32
Carbeth changes	33
Rock-A-Bye Baby	34
The Story	36
something funny	38
Being Seen	39

Quicksilver Thoughts

Quicksilver thoughts	43
Easdale New Year	44
When You've Been Away	46
The Space Between	47

I Come With Big White Flowers	48
Not Knowing	49
Dumgoyach	50
The big Buddha	51
not waking up	52
the first	53
to mist	54

Dancing with the Hyacinths

Dancing with the Hyacinths	57
On the edge	58
You are here	59
Ana Creagan Ridge Walk	60
During the hospital visit	62
I am waiting for you to give birth	63
Nappyless in Regent's Park	64
Electric Pony	65
Return to Glasgow	66
Barbican at 6 weeks	68
last night in Berlin	69
Kilmartin	70
The Wedding Day	71
gathering of crows	72

London to Kilmackerin West

London to Kilmackerin West	75
Dance from Kilmackerin West	80
a pretty girl	81
First teacher	82
unspoken intimacy	84
"Things I Learned Last Week"	85

Notes

*wishing you alive
we bowed in four directions
then gave-up your ghost*

After the bones

After the bones

After returning your mobile phone
and briefly speaking about our son
leaving home, cycling across town
warm for the beginning of October
sweating on arrival at the hospital

after teaching in the physio gym
the art students painting on the floor
in the Collins gallery, waiting to be seen
at the housing benefit office then stillness
in booth two, the computer screen
saver throbs with slim stripes of colour

after an appointment at the dentist
no queuing at the co-operative bank
smiling in the wholefood shop I buy
a loaf of 100% rye, soya milk, cous-cous
cakes and pakora from the deli

after eating an apple a filling falls out
then meeting John cycling along the river
telling me his father died yesterday:

everything changes after that.
pedalling hard uphill the crunch
of beechnuts under my tyres
reminds me of bones.

that sounds like the beginning of a poem

At dinner tonight I almost bit my tongue
but I stopped myself just before I did it.

Then I proudly said to everyone (there were
twenty of us at table):

*I almost bit my tongue but I stopped
myself just before I did it.*

Then you said:

*that sounds like the beginning of a poem.
a poem a poem*

So I said it again louder:

***I almost bit my tongue but I stopped
myself just before I did it.***

Everyone laughed so later I wrote: *at dinner
tonight I almost bit my tongue but I stopped
myself just before I did it.*

Butterfly Bones

The sun on your head warms your butterfly bones.
Where will you fly today exhaling ten thousand moans,
How many moon flowers will you penetrate with no seed
no stamen, no nectar, no stones, no subject, no need
and not meaning to fly apart, not wrong and not right?
It is early spring and the buds are tight.
Ice on the puddle, your brain's in a muddle. Can you
open your heart so only this moment shines,
so nothing gets in the way when exhaling rhymes
and you are left with a free hand floating blue
off the page without fancy words or funny turns?
Laying fragrant eggs between your ears, when you burn
smoke will rise and you will hear silent cheers from a Christian
congregation of crows; when your red-black wings flutter
ready now, steady now, free from clutter
you will land on a dry dead branch of beech
hanging like a pendulum above the bog –
ideal for the fire and a blue flaming dialogue.

Goodnight Kisses

if I could remember
what I dreamed, I would
dismember it, send you
the remains together with
goodnight kisses.

>   *you telephoned very early
>   this morning, you said
>   that he was dead. very
>   dead.   the cancer got
>   his liver.*

ok. but what if
you didn't know him
never sucked his ears,
what then? not, I hope
the plain song, not another
Mrs. or near miss, mis-
taken images. The mis-
sing person could be you
who lack your quota of orgasms.

>   *"the church has a lot to answer for",
>   **forever** for example, and forgetting
>   disease until you can't shit anymore.*

The lesson
is not to eat
less unless/until
you delight in fragmented messages
from sleep and dark kisses before,
after, then goodbye/never for example

> *not hanging*
> *up the phone*
> *it went dead too*
> *hung from the cord*
> *spinning counter clockwise*
> *two inches from the floor*

Hindrance

*She often talks to me during meditation
about why she committed suicide*

Maybe I'm frightened of your perpetual wise smile
    thank goodness there's no light in here
so I could see that you were only pretending
    To have right answers to all my questions,

and I am frightened of your all knowing smile
    that might reveal the truth about me:
perhaps I don't want to be contented.
    All change, yours sincerely, all change

from catty grins to jumping heebeegeebees –
    thank goodness we have candles
so we can play with our shadows when it's dark.
    No I don't know what it is,

perhaps your silly plastic face
    when you're about to jump
down my throat with a bright torch
    determined to find out what's wrong.

That's it though, there is nothing
    just a dull thud-thud, thud-thud
inhaling black, exhaling white, then wheezing,
    you wishing my smile flourished like sweet peas,

but my brain is slow, depressed, imploded
    in dark corners with frown wrinkles down to my toes.
Are you with me, do you ken now
    how frightened I was of your perpetual wise smirk?

Thank goodness for the uselessness of this carnival,
    but oh how necessary sometimes to fling
and forget myself in a panic, a frenetic desire to run
    and hide in a cupboard, drink whisky forever.

stale memory

Sitting on the potty
with you holding me down till I shat –
it doesn't matter anymore
but you did that.
And you tried to do it again,
I caught you at it –
you were enthusiastic
holding my 2-year-old son
forcing him to sit on the potty.
He had a look of surprise,
didn't seem to mind.
It mattered then to me.
I stopped you.
I told you never to do that again.
Now you don't have access to children.
Now my son is an adult. I will not
hold his child down on the potty.
The memory is stale. Now I hold
your wrinkled arm, weak and flabby,
as we wobble up the stairs
to watch the telly.

Mother Crosswords

Consider a morning with your mother
beginning at dawn as the sky brightens.
Notice the slight breeze, cooking smells,
the lay of clouds folding into each other.

You drink green tea, she drinks green tea
and reads the paper aloud and the TV's loud too.
She thinks you want to hear about the tight
race in the November election. You want to spew.

She has considered stopping the paper.
There are forty-six television stations to choose
from, but she would miss turning the pages
even when she can't see the print, she can muse

and moan about the weather and the democrats.
The clouds unfold as the sun streams into the room.
She closes the blinds to protect her glaucoma eyes,
surfs the channels till she finds a suitable groom,

someone, anyone but you, to drone away the hours,
the fifteen years since her husband, your father,
left his body pickled with whisky, eaten by cancer.
She asks you questions to fill spaces in crosswords.

negative capability

when a man is capable of being in uncertainties, mysteries, doubts, without irritable reaching after fact and reason.

Head banging the wall
I hide in a corner
trying to be invisible
then I flop around
pretending to be a seal.

I stole your cigarettes
I stole your liquor
added water to the bottle
so you wouldn't notice.

You beat me so often
it was one more thing you did
one more thing you didn't do.
Beat the boy – just another job
you did as you were told
doing what was done to you.

Mom kept score
while you were at work:
never less than three whacks,
sometimes more than ten.

A father's duty, you made
a big paddle for hitting me:
a flat two-foot piece of laminated ply,
3 inches by 1 inch thick
tapered to a leather handle
the size of your grip. You drilled
six half-inch-wide holes so
you could swing it faster

I never let you know it hurt.
It hurt. Welts festered
in my piss when I wet the bed.

When I saw a film
about men clubbing seal pups
it reminded me of you.

You were the first to teach me
negative capability: to empty myself
of any visible reaction.

How do I approach you now,
17 years after you died?
We saw so little of each other.

I wish it were different.

Frogs at the Funeral

Grandpa at Grandma's funeral,
head bowed, a sob jumps from his throat.
Unexpected and sudden another frog leaps
as Grandpa lunges forward to her coffin
followed by his two sons. My father
holds him on one side, Uncle Bob the other,
as a steady stream of frogs
creep from the lump in his throat,
then leap from his mouth,
each with a wild croak.

Grandpa's hands scratch the mahogany inlay.
Agony rolls in his dry eyes as he
clenches and unclenches his fist.
He swallows a frog.
He gasps.
He holds down his vomit.
Silent sobs echoed off stained glass,
our pain absorbed by deep red velvet curtains.

Later that Summer we play cribbage
in the late evening with cicadas
slapping the windows, numbers float
in the lamplight 15 / 2 15 / 4 and a pair
of threes for 6 – 15 / 2 15 / 4 15 / 6 and
a run of three for 9, with long pauses
between deals, while the pears and plums
rot on the trees.

He stops hoeing weeds.
He stops sowing seeds.
He stops fishing at dawn.
He stops turning the compost heap.
He stops feeding the ducks.
He stops feeding the hens.
He stops collecting eggs.
He stops digging for worms.
He stops playing horseshoes.

After dinner, we play cribbage
with cicadas slapping the windows.

That Summer of '62, the lake died
from an overdose of chemical spray
designed to kill gnats. 10,000 big fish
 (the ones he dreamt of catching
    the ones that got away)
floated to the surface with their silvery
white bloated bellies skyward,
their stink hung in the warm air.

He stops going to church.
He stops speaking to neighbours.
He stops speaking to me.

Numbers float in the lamplight:
15 / 2 15 / 4 and a double run for twelve
15 / 2 15 / 4 15 / 6 and three 7s for twelve
15 / 2 15 / 4 15 / 6 and a double double run
for 18.

He stopped going out.
He stopped sleeping.
He sold the farm, went walk about.
He walked about followed by an impotent bull frog.

He walked from relative to relative:
Florida, Georgia, Indiana, Illinois,
until a stroke
made him choke.
Then he leaped into her grave
and the frogs in his throat
went to sleep.

The phlebotomist

Every morning the phlebotomist takes my blood,
in the afternoon the nurse gives me suppositories
but your rant on the phone about a sneaky journalist
that is my real medicine, gives meaning to my pain.

Every morning the assistant takes my blood pressure,
twice a day she attaches a bag of antibiotics to drip
into my veins. Can I respect this pain? I don't know.

I don't know what's wrong with me. They don't know
what's wrong with me. Whatever it is it must be good,
why judge it as bad? Anything could kill me

even these words but tell me your angry story
and I will soak it into my guts and feel better.

This morning the consultant doctor asked a student
why she was late – "I like excuses" he said.
"I slept in" she said. "Honesty is good, the ward
round starts at 8, you've missed all the gems".

I don't think I'm one of the gems.

Lines on the River

Your dry eyes reveal a deeper depression than anyone realised.
                Who said you were alive today?

Please remember to clean your ears before you go
        to another concert. What are these half-heard un-sung notes

forgotten so quickly as you gaze at the heron's slow movement
            after the sudden death of a grasshopper

rescued from the road? So green! So still & vital. Carefully
    cupped in your right palm, opening your hand

over the brambles, he struts on your life lines displaying
        fearless dexterity, then hops off to apparent freedom

directly into a spider's web. Holding your breath, unblinking,
            you witness the deadly bite –

killed instantly by the patient resident. Was it painless?
        Is she grateful for your unintended act of generosity?

Dark grooves on your forehead photograph surprise valleys
        of perplexity while generations of anguish expire

from your open mouth. Will grasshopper benefit in some future
        life from such fleeting human contact?

With a nail file, you separate the victim from his natural enemy.
    You delay the feast. Now a fish leaps and the heron's more still

and half the willow branches droop beneath the dark water.
              What is that moisture on your cheeks as the sun peeks

below grey pillows? Who knows why death is so sudden so still
    and absolute. Just after the bite he curls into a tiny green ball

the size of an unripe blackcurrant. The heron's long neck so long.
              Midges hover, more fish jump. Sentinels of purple

flowers line the water's edge singing like angels
      as meandering cows munch forever in the background

beyond grey and black ripples. And that hill on the horizon
        is the only still and static message from your volcanic past.

Real revolutionaries stay at home

& mend holes in jumpers
    weaving thru patterns
    that are already there
warp & weft while wishing
for a better world: watching the leaves
turn yellow then red then fall.

You need to know how to knit a jumper
before you can mend it, they are made
from the bottom up so you
unravel from the top down.
What does this say about politics:
start by toppling the people on top

with power to begin mending from
   the bottom rising up thru the pattern.
Some jumpers breed holes
great gaps in the conversation,
slips of tongue Left, Right & Centre
forgetting how to make good.

The longer you leave a hole
the harder it is to mend –
    your faults made visible
    knowing you are vulnerable
& capable of so many mistakes.
Recognising faults as strengths

your patches could be a feature,
a quilt reducing your guilt
about not doing enough
                for the world.

Baking Bread

Late afternoon kneading
kneading the dough. You
were mumbling to yourself
then you said   out loud:

> *she's a good dog*
> *but not a good hunter.*

> *maybe Rita will take her.*

Outside
it's getting dark

flour
    water
        sticky fingers)))

a car brakes   screech

    sound of bone
on   metal
        crushing .

And you said:
> *maybe Rita will take her.*

Buried in   the garden
near   the hives, she will
protect   the bees.

Rising dough

    spreading the   blood
    with   buckets of water

        She's a good dog
        but not a good hunter,

        Rita's husband shoots animals
        doesn't much like dogs

Baking bread
the oven doesn't get hot enough
so it will be a thin crust.

the anger will endure
in language strict and pure

As I sit emptying my bowels
with some considerable pain
while reading a standard form poem
by Theodore Roethke: "the anger will endure…
in a language strict and pure"
my belly smiles certain that the flush
will cure a constipated brain.
Today life seems so short
when we meet in Safeways:

we dawdle from aisle to aisle
trying to remember
what we came in for –

our sons rollerblade
between *cereals & household*

"I will reheat yesterday's Shepherd Pie
boil corn-on-the-cob
slice raw carrot and cucumber…

Yesterday life seemed so short
I feel so tired today, how are you?"

Crinan

At Crinan Ferry our campfire burns through the rain as we cook the chanterelles we quietly poached yesterday evening on a hill behind a castle while the laird had his tea.

> Oh 1000 chanterelles
> more golden than daffodils
>
> these rare fish on greenhills
> hide in an old caledonian wood
>
> Muffling our giggles of delight
> we poach enough for now and tomorrow
> then wash them in the sea by the castle
> the salt will bring out their flavour
>
> Ahh a basket full of chanterelles,
> their scent is indescribable.

Four of us huddle over one pot. We munch & lick our lips & smile through the rain.

The neighbour's telly's too loud.

The upstairs neighbour's telly's too loud.
It's late. The upstairs neighbour's telly's too loud.
It's late. The upstairs neighbour's telly's too loud. I can't meditate.
It's late. The upstairs neighbour's telly's too loud. I can't meditate.
I can't write.
It's late. The upstairs neighbour's telly's too loud. I can't think. I can't meditate. I can't write.
It's late. The upstairs neighbour's telly's too loud. I can't think. I can't meditate. I can't write. Tell them to turn it off.
It's late. The upstairs neighbour's telly's too loud. I can't think. I can't meditate. I can't write. Tell them to turn it off. No you tell them to turn it off.
It's late. The upstairs neighbour's telly's too loud. I can't think. I can't meditate. I can't write. Tell them to turn it off. No you tell them to turn it off. It's your turn.
It's late. The upstairs neighbour's telly's too loud. I can't think. I can't meditate. I can't write. Tell them to turn it off. No you tell them to turn it off. It's your turn. Please.
It's very late. The upstairs neighbour's telly's too loud. I can't think. I can't meditate. I can't write. I can't sleep. Tell them to turn it off. No you tell them to turn it off. It's your turn. Please go tell them to turn it off.
It's very late, the upstairs neighbour's telly was too loud. They've gone to bed. I can't think. I can't meditate. I can't write. I can't sleep. It's your turn. Please go tell them to turn it on.

57 All Saints Road

Inside and out
    your whole house
   sings with abundance:
ready for rituals,
     carved coloured sticks
     stand upright in corners
and paper wings
   cling to the ceiling
and your thousands of books,
pictures and photos
   fill the walls –
     more books and papers
        pile on the stairs.
There's a meadow in the back
and a wild hedge at the front
       conceals your entrance
just like your bush of a beard
       reminds me of Whitman.

Upper Ostaig House

For Jules, Chris, Winnie, Stella, Arthur

Breathing in cool mist
breathing out warm air
we walk the empty path

        talking little –
        uphill holding hands

"Darf ich dich küssen?"
"Ja, mit vergnügen."
Not much is needed to be happy:

        silence at the summit
        red sky over the Cuillins.

our clothes flap in the wind,
as we slurp green soup then
slip between clean white sheets.

        rain soaked lesser spotted orchid
        and tormentil along the spongy path

Nude in peat water,
a fall onto mossy forest floor –
midges keep us moving.

        when its hot and breezy
        we sleep easy on sea-smoothed rock.

meditating with roses
we wake-up to the passing
of pleasure and pain:

"Froh zu sein bedarf es wenig"
    so why can't we just let go?

On the day of departure
a spinning washing machine
penetrates our spines –

        insulin injection before porridge
        & a ritual: cleaning the porch window.

With sugar levels too high
we beam over coffee
eager for one last dance

    down to the beach
    where gulls cry and seals bark.

18 movements inhaling the tide
exhaling 10 days together
where lochs mirror mountains,

    after a long low note on the flute
    we reflect on nothing in particular for half an hour.

Now with full belly
we thank our friends on Mingulay
for the loan of their house on Skye:

    curled on the chair by the aga
    two black cats await their return.

                (with Ratnadevi)

constipated in the USA

The morphine did that.
You liked being regular,
ordinary
a daily release, relief.

Now you are dying.
I think you know that
you are dying
    but you pretend
to be getting better
with vertical spine
upright, standing tall,
    strong
even in your last days

but constipated –
and you hate that
curled on the toilet
    straining
like a dog. I rub
your belly, stroke your back.

You strain to be well
and I wait
and you wait
till I'm over the Atlantic
before going into a coma.

I hold my breath as you die
before the plane lands in Scotland.

Bones

Elizabeth
Liz, Lizzy, Lisa
Tree woman
Mountain woman
   bella crone,
Good witch
   Bad witch
Ho down hag:
Shy as a fish,
Bold four winds –
Your words fly
Into the mouths of demons as
a bear,
Mother of stories,
Maker of stone –
carved letters
Thrown to the four winds –
And goddesses devour
Your characters.

    Lisa, sweet Lisa
  Queen of Disguise
  hiding your bones
  has made you wise

Lisa now
Lizzy then
Liz was Elizabeth:
You are instigator,
Alligator, collaborator,
Feminine warrior,
   friendly foe,
     of birth and death
     and the truth
as only you can tell it.
fondly remembered
   fairy godmother –
Lady MacBeth
   with your dark veil,
   I stand before you
   trembling, pale,
Haunted by memories

Lisa, sweet Lisa
  Queen of Disguise
  hiding your bones
  has made you wise
  10,000 scenarios
  you have shapes
  where the terrible
    became touchable
  chewed and soothed
  by seamless silk
    narratives.
Your many voices
untangle knots
of fear and grief
releasing lightning
bolts of laughter –
applauding storms.

Lisa, sweet Lisa
Queen of disguise
hiding your bones
has made you wise

Lisa hear my wish
that you trust your blood.
Hear my prayer
  that you become
  bolder, stronger,
  stranger
with each coming year:
Honking. Hawking.
Cracking your lines
  and charms
in Leicester, Glasgow, London
New York, Sheffield, New Zealand –
Everywhere
May your words
    bounce off the moon
Scattering magic notes
   with silver tones.
    Lisa sweet Lisa
   Queen of disguise
  hiding your bones
has made you wise

Forty Years On

Two hawks hover and hunt
over the Kendal Hills, their cry cuts
through the continuous whirr of the M6
like your humorous tone lightens a heavy heart.

Clouds turn pink as you skip and slide
along an icy lane whistling a forgotten tune
with a herd of sheep at your heels
hoping your rucksack is filled with turnips.

Walking backwards you see
what has been before you knew how
to put wings in your voice, when you heard
a human cry in the waterfall by Fawcette Mill.

Two hawks hover and hunt
over the Kendal Hills, one hawk dives:
the mouse's heart stops and as you turn round twice,
blinking, these four days become forty years.

Carbeth changes

schmirrs of bluebells on the hills
makes me smile on the bus.

There's a new gate with birch posts
        and a bigger woodpile
five apple trees all have leaves
        two have pink blossom
and you've cut the grass to mark a path
        from tree to tree to hut to hedge
and pruned the hedge by the rowan unearthing an old gate
        three birch logs mark a bonfire place
chives, oregano, and sage grow in an urn
        protected from the deer by a metal cage.
your rhubarb flourishes.
        The kitchen's newly painted yellow
and the backroom has a roof,
        a mirror over the sink with two brass candle holders
lights your face
        a towel horse, another table, a chest of drawers
and a re-vamped ash drawer for the stove
        windows washed, mirror by the bed settee
and in a small brown box magnetic games
        of ludo, chess, and draughts for long winter nights.

Rock-A-Bye Baby

    In the glen near Ballycarry on Red Hall Estate
where orchids grow near madman's leap   a water
fall   falls

Here is where the Ulster Defence Regiment practice
their war games   some years ago the UDA
played here too   until
the security forces booted them out   OUT

Here is where the flags are placed   for a motor cycle
rally   every Saturday afternoon

    And here I am walking with a baby   smelling
orchids   and talking about what I can do to prevent
the government from selling   Red Hall Estate
I will pose as a wealthy American and offer millions
of dollars for this property   then make it known
to the public that here I will build   a poison factory
which will kill   everyone who complains
about anything   the government dare not accept
my offer   pigfools they are   they will be forced
to preserve this land   plant more flowers and trees

we will run wild shouting our dreams   dancing
in the rain   we will sing all night and roast potatoes
not people   a sandpit there   fishpond here
gooseberries   rabbits   flying red squirrels   rhubarb
raspberries   hedgehogs   mushrooms   toads   elvers

    my voice has lulled the baby to sleep in the glen
near Ballycarry   where the Ulster Defence Regiment
practised and played   a water fall   falls
near madman's leap   LEAP

The Story

1. Hello Yes...No...in the Botanics?!...really!...in the middle of the day!...I would have screamed...Why did you stop?...You didn't...Did he touch you?...How big was it?...My God!...a cleaver...really!...Oh how could you, I could've never done that...you certainly were lucky...I would've given it to him straight away...was he Scottish?...Glaswegian...couldn't you tell?...Ok I'll meet you at the Metro at half past two.

✦✦✦

2. I'm walking down the steps by Kelvin Way. down. down. down them steps with rain dripping off bare branches thudding on my brolly. Thud. Thud. Thud. On the bridge, you ask me the time: "Have ya got the time Miss?" on the white bridge you ask me the time. I hear the ducks: quack quack quack. I hear the robin. "1.36" I say – you look lost – I think. Black eye, short-cropped hair, pink anorak, early twenties, lost, you look lost. I'm on my way to the bank to pay in one hundred and fifty pounds cash – in an envelope – in my rucksack – I don't believe it – in my rucksack, in my rucksack is one hundred and fifty pounds cash. over the bridge I turn round. You wave and say: "Is this the Botanics...which way do I go?" You walk towards me. I pause. pause. pause. You are lost I think you are lost. lost. lost. Quite close now – a meter away – you reveal from under your coat a kitchen knife, a cleaver. cleaver. cleaver. "Gimme yr bag" you say in a quiet faltering voice while gesturing towards me with the knife. You look left right left right left right. Your eyes wander like a frightened squirrel. I step back. "Don't move" you say. "Don't be silly" I say. "Don't do this, I'm not going to give you my bag." my bag. my bag. He says: "You're lucky this time." He turns and runs runs runs up the steps to Botanic Crescent. I run run run up the steps – pink anorak – into the gardens – short

cropped hair – as another man walks down the steps deep in his own thoughts oblivious of my situation. I phone the police from a shop in Byres Rd.

✦✦✦

3. "Tell me what happened." I walked down the steps to the river; as I crossed the white bridge into the Botanics, a man asked me the time. "What was the time?" 1:36. He looked lost. "What did he look like? Describe him." A black eye, short hair – dirty blond – dark pink anorak, dark with rain. After crossing the bridge I turned to look at him. He waved to me. I walked towards him. He walked towards me. When he got close he asked me if this was the Botanic Gardens. Then he pulled a knife. "Which hand?" Left hand. "What kind of knife?" A square kitchen knife – a cleaver. "Did he threaten you?" He held it close to his side and just kept saying "gimme yr bag, gimme yr bag" while pushing the knife towards me. He looked left and right and behind, his eyes wandering like a frightened animal. I stepped back. "Don't move," he said. "Don't be silly, don't do this. I'm not going to give you my bag…" I said. I felt stronger than him. He was nervous, not sure of himself. "Yr lucky this time." He said as he turned and ran over the bridge and up the steps to Botanic Crescent. I don't remember what sort of trousers, I didn't notice his shoes. Smaller than me. Black eye. Square kitchen knife. "Scottish?" yes Scottish. "Glaswegian?" yes Glaswegian accent. I phoned the police from a shop in Byres Road.

✦✦✦

4. I will walk down the steps to the River Kelvin. On the bridge to the Botanics, a man will ask me the time. He will have a black eye and look a bit lost. As I look at my watch – 1:36 – it will fall off my wrist into the river. That's all I remember.

something funny

something funny, odd, peculiar
heard or seen recently?

thinking of something funny
is like telling me to have fun.

the cat's in the sink purring
as the tap drips on his fur.

Being Seen

so you think you see me
you can't see me not really
you only pretend to see me
its all in your imagination
no one ever sees me   I hide
even out in the open I'm an
invisible shadow safely camouflaged
like a pheasant sitting on her eggs
no one will ever see me or will they

will I let you see me   who sees me
sees nothing   will I give you permission
to see me   completely   what do I fear
being found out   what will you find out
perhaps there's nothing to me   you'll look
and look and look and you'll see nothing

there's nothing to see
I don't exist   I pretend
to be here but I'm elsewhere   absent
unborn disembodied skirting the galaxy
I float in a time warp of faded memory
seen unseen   seen again

Quicksilver Thoughts

for Rd

Quicksilver thoughts

Quicksilver thoughts slip from brain to heart to hand
out fingertips to pen, wet with inconclusive stammers
and bright stabs of understatement longing to be voiced

proud to exist even without lip to shape the wriggly mass
into digestible forms. Indecisive grunts roll out and spread
all over the blank universe: "Look at me! Hear me! Taste me!

Love me! Lift me! Make me! Wait for me!" they scream
they whisper they challenge and push forward incessantly
demanding undivided attention for unambiguous meaning.

If only there were enough words. If only words had enough
sound to make sense when action speeds silver particles
of pure existence that float away quicker than imagination.

Easdale New Year

Through squall and sleet
by black water a robin
leads you to a gale force swell:
snow on Mull and clouds swirl
above slate-washed shores
gulls cry
over white water
              the faint Paps of Jura

your arms fold in dark blue
weather proofs – a bright blue cap and gloves –
swish of pvc and teeth of waves

blue – grey – gold sky
tunnels of light
spill on dark water
A peewit squeals
              over faint Paps of Jura

bones of a dinosaur:
leafless spiky curves of bramble
we harvested the main crop in September

between lichen-covered stones
moss and rusty heather
shiver in gusts of wind
while a canvas-wrapped sculpture
lashed with rope (it was nude in June)

alone in a walled garden
surrounded by a skeleton of clematis
stories waft in white smoke
and a bouquet of green-yellow
orange-red and blue-black buoys
dangle from the coal shed.

When You've Been Away

When you've been away
for a weekend, a week or longer
and I hear the keys in the lock
and I know that you are home
I pretend not to notice
or it could be me coming home
and you pretend not to notice
but this time it's you. I sit
quietly in the front room
facing the bay window overlooking
the Kelvin – the setting sun glows
across the carpet. I quietly read
aloud a poem by Ian or Tom
or Mary or Elizabeth or Bill.
I hear your rucksack clunk to the floor,
the hall cupboard door opens and closes.
Not long now I'm thinking
and there's a tingling in my spine.
I feel you looking at me, your eyes
on the back of my neck. I don't move
and I continue reading silently. You step
into the room, sit at the piano and begin
to play Mozart. I stop reading. Stand.
Turn and look at the back of your neck
admire your perfect posture. I part the air
with my arms and roll along the carpet
until I am looking up into your face. You
concentrate on the music until the end. I roll away
and you follow me, I follow you, you follow me
mirroring and mocking with shocks of recognition
we re-fashion our segregated lives.

The Space Between

in the space   be
tween   the trees
where   the river
flows   narrow
and   shallow
yesterday   there was
a heron   a heron
fishing   but today
the elder   blooms
and I   will soak
the white blossom in water
to quench
my love's
thirst

I Come With Big White Flowers

I come with big white flowers
snow white hair wearing galoshes
hot smiles raring to kiss everything

Bowlegged I swagger across the   room
dribbling on the carpet

You gently touch my shoulder

Holy   Unhinged   Standard Lamp!

My tea leaves come true
the cat counts the chickens
before they hatch   You are my ground

coffee   weetabix   biscuits and oh
won't you please

just gorgeous the geranium

Not Knowing

What kills me

is not knowing

                      everything

all the time   and not having you

                    always   all ways

and you

wanting more now   knowing

that having everything   I want

                    leaves me wanting

nothing   so naturally

                      all I want

                      is you   now

                    and always

                  /

nothing is left   then

for me to want   if you

want me

too

Dumgoyach

that wooded knoll
that fairy hill of pure basalt
by the West Highland Way
formed by the mouth of a volcano
where purple mushrooms grow
where roe deer hide
where we made love
on a mossy ridge overlooked
by the Kilpatrick hills

The big Buddha

between us smiles
and in your eyes
I see tears from
100,000 years.

this spring morning
in our silk gowns
the frieze of sweet days

quietly longing
for sweet tranquillity –
for the embodiment
of peace,

I consciously
subscribe and imitate
that unfathomable gaze

not waking up

Early this morning   before dawn   a rough sky
scraping the window   I grope down the stairs

                wide awake
              on a cold toilet seat
                still dreaming

Back in our smallish bed
        warming my feet on your legs
while watching the clouds turn pink
adjusting the blankets   a comfortable battle
      then sleep

         glimpse
         of an earlier dream
                  /
                            gliding

At noon I blink   nothing is blue   thick
grey clouds   nor bright   the frosty
quiet houses   Sunday droops

                only
        the seagull's vigorous flight
              disturbs

the first

She lived in Willow Ranch
Across Cottle Avenue
Next to the mayor's house.

June's when we romped thru
Orchards & vineyards
Searching for a place to love
Enclosed by blossoms.

to mist
rising

to seagulls
rinsing
salt from feathers

to clouds
clinging
to hills

to you & me
yawning
stretching

to birds
flapping
thru clouds

to mist
drifting
in sunrise

to kisses
like this
like this
and this

Dancing with the Hyacinths

Dancing with the Hyacinths

for Freya

They lean towards the window.
For balance we turn them round
and more pink fragrance in the room.

During the day, rising slowly to attention,
they lean towards the window,
we turn them round for balance
and more pink fragrance in the room.

Overnight they wait still and poised
on the table in the dark until dawn.
While we sleep, they rise slowly with the sun
then lean towards the window
dropping pink petals on the sill.

For balance we turn them round
and more pink fragrance in the room.
We turn round as they turn round

until dizzy as a dervish we fall
until tired and spent they droop.

On the edge

Tongue tied behind upper front teeth
lips open close open close open
as if about to speak something

important but no words come out.
On the edge of knowing what to say
there's a moan a mumble a pause

at the end of the in-breath swallowing
clearing the throat ready for the right
words pre-prepared with an exclamation

affirming the edge between knowing
and not knowing what exactly to say –
that's when we most need to listen.

You are here

    with words showing themselves
shining dark & soft like shy moles
come out come out and say it
    that lively word beyond compare
    that sound making perfect sense
    that crinkle that clears the air
    that glad phrase that sings
along the path thru nettles unstung
    let us assume it is here apparent
it is here   you are here not *were*
not *will be*   you are here
    like the map tells us
    with an arrow
you are here with me
burning ever so slowly
    the wood that was a tree
    the wax that was a candle
    the flowers that were outside
    now in a green vase
on a persian carpet pleasing
the inside air feathering
the silence by staring
  out the window wishing
  you could join the birds
singing their effortless tunes
fly away free forgetting
    whatever you had to say
when you were here

Ana Creagan Ridge Walk

A gathering of words along the way
Sunday 23rd October 2005

James, Duncan, Larry
with Kevin in the lead
crunching up the stony path
sweating in the dreich
as water pours down

full of chatter & good cheer
the deer climb higher

quiet on the bealch
in the lea below the summit
in each other's footsteps
over white/green dolerite
grey andacite pink thyolite

Kevin tells us the MacDonald
burial island is overcrowded

on Am Bodach we rope up
wearing a harness like a girdle
James' mother's guts would come out
if she didn't wear one Dr. Duncan doesn't
ask older women to belly breathe

a cairn at the entrance to Glen Coe
held a MacDonald body overnight

belching stags & munchies
on the ridge   slipping over scree
a boot wedged between rocks
along the top scratching
the back of a buffalo

frozen grasses form silent letters
wind direction's on the icy side

hoar frost on the Chancellor
squeals of snow bunting
where does your left foot go
secure in the mist because
we can't see the long drops

watch out for loose rocks when
the slack goes start climbing

when you get up take care
of the guy behind   when the
mist clears on Meall Dearg
even here 900 meters above
the road cars whirr & whoosh

reindeer moss swells the stomach
men survived on it for 3 months

too late for blueberries on Stob
Coire Leith   drink lady's mantle tea
for fertility & prevent saggy breasts
already changed from brown to grey
& white 3 ptarmigans take off west

to Sgorr nam Fiannai where we descend
following the lead of a hare

During the hospital visit

our baby squirms in your belly.
What can I do, I want to fly
away? Will it survive, be ok
die young?
         I could climb mountains

while I wait, our child squirms
in your belly but maybe it's a lie
not the sky heavy with traffic smell –
will it ever come – come & go my
         dream of clean air and

easy to write poems) our baby
squirms in your belly, my father
retired from General Electric after
producing billions of pellets of uranium –
         they gave him a clock.

Already separate the pain's not
within me, our baby squirms in
your belly while my feet outside
walk on concrete. I want to scream
         but the pain's not within me –
your breasts grow big.

I am waiting for you to give birth
The tomatoes are ripening on the roof

I am waiting for myself to begin work
The radishes have gone to seed on the roof

I am waiting for the world to end
The endives are flowering on the roof

I am waiting for a pause in the traffic
The marrows grow big and rot on the roof

I am waiting for colours to turn white
The spinach is wilting brown on the roof

I am waiting for sleep to finish the day
Rain rains, thunder thunders on the roof

I am waiting so long I've forgotten what for
Wet tiles, sodden earth in white sinks on the roof

I am waiting for the sun or maybe my daughter

Nappyless in Regent's Park

you sit on Barbara Hepworth
flesh banging on hollow metal
you kiss
    slobber slurp trying
to find out who she is
by hiding in her curves
and we gab all day: "aga aga"
while her silent gesture
speaks to passing clouds
    she leaves no mark
you scratch & pull at my tit
but I have no milk – I am a man.
Barbara's history is a mystery.
    your piss may give her rust.

Electric Pony

for Ossian

In the cafe a toddler canters
on a 20p wooden electric pony
with tight brow & boss-eyed
she scowls sticks her tongue
out at the queue of children de-
termined no one else gets a shot
she puts another 20p in the slot
& another & again at a steady pace
proud stiff lips on her little old face.

Return to Glasgow

19 weeks 133 days without words
not one poem since leaving London
few letters, but many stuffed birds
live in the Kelvingrove Museum.

Copper and silver tiles line our bathroom,
each with a different engraving: song thrush, rook,
bean goose, tawny owl, capercaillie, heron, snipe
(I've decided not to join the local birdwatching club)

Our year-old son wants to hear each name
10,000 times. The rhymes are hard,
some say Glasgow's dour. My claim
for unemployment benefit has stopped

the drain on our small savings,
one evening class brings in £15.00 a week.
Steak and kidney pudding's your pregnant craving,
we will have another baby in July.

Since leaving London 134 days past,
after a Chinese meal in Tottenham Court Road,
the pram piled high with precious last thoughts
of jugs, plants, clean nappies and Scottish stones –

baby on your back, pack on my back,
the wheels squeak from Regents Park to Euston
then we sleep in a sleeper, dream into the crack
widening the gap and the tracks between houses.

Glasgow has pigeons too. Chinese ducks quack
on the frozen pond in Kelvingrove Park
littered with realistic sculpture, our son is quick
to distinguish the living from the dead.

Barbican at 6 weeks

Crispy blue bright morning
biking with you asleep on my chest

we weave through traffic
along the Gray's Inn Road watched

by the bark-bark, bark-bark
behind barbed wire of building sites.

We bark back at the roaring cars
rushing to work, wave at shopkeepers

unlocking doors as the real business
begins. We soar with a song softening

the streets of London and laugh when
my left pedal sticks.

last night in Berlin

waiting for the dark
sun ribbons sparkle
across the water

Venus in orange light
above the woods
Mars above the poplars

Jupiter's moon
almost visible

a new moon splashes
in the river

a candlelit meal
on the veranda
toasting the universe

Kilmartin

A generator fills the silence of this empty church. The one-thousand-year-old stones of Christ stand in awe of each other.
These slabs are symbols of self glory and heraldic fame:

>17 animals
>16 swords
>7 knights
>1 fish
>1 boat
>1 bishop
>1 womanly saint

We compete to find these forty-four carved images framed in celtic patterns in a glassed-in sepulchre, a tribute to Iain Cambeul and his mate. Three boys play hide and seek in the grave yard. Ten years ago while hitch-hiking from Kerry to Iona, I slept in a derelict house opposite, a cold night and I was a bit scared, reminded me of another empty house on the outskirts of Chicago in '64 hitching my way with Judy to Antioch, Ohio. Am I here, with you singing alone, the lord's prayer, as if this church were full of a private royal wedding? I found them:

>1 womanly saint (that's you)
>1 bishop (that's not me)
>1 boat
>1 fish
>7 knights
>16 swords
>17 animals

The Wedding Day

after rain
the broom pops
in the warm sun

the guests gather
for the wedding feast

a neighbour pauses
from weeding
to pick the first
ripe brambles

the host swims
in the bride's womb

the groom plays
a drum   pauses
to hear the broom
pop and crack
in the warm sun

the host gathers
the guests to swim
in the bride's womb

   they dance
   to strip the willow

gathering of crows

how to die
how to live
how to love

bumping into Tina in the park
in her wheelchair with her helper Gloria
from Stoke-on-Trent
then Jack came along and Gerry
there we were   a gathering of crows
cawing over pistachio nuts
chewing the wind
soaking up the afternoon sun
a party with bananas pakora and chocolate
Gloria rolled a cigarette
kindly sat downwind
we talked about

how to die quickly
how to live simply
a long breath in
longing for more
longing for love

along comes Karen
7½ months pregnant
a glorious battle inside her
so we all jump in
and save the day

London to Kilmackerin West

London to Kilmackerin West

Pack for Ireland   rush to catch the train to Wales
no time to buy a ticket   little money   I hide in the loos

Michael's on the boat   casual tall slim dark-skinned
American Italian trumpet player from Seattle   friend of Jon
the drummer

long nonstop rap about his journey meditating on pedals up
and down the Welsh hills with black plastic bags wrapped
around his calves and ankles

                        on deck
                        in my sleeping bag
                        sea gulls float
                        in the wake
                        under a half moon

Docking   goodbye Michael   goodbye sea   goodbye
boat   hello Ireland   hello Ireland   I'm here   I'm here in
Ireland   here in Ireland   here I am in Ireland   and I want
a lift   to Kerry   I want a lift to Kerry   I want a lift to Kerry
is there anyone going my way   my way   the free way   the
long and the short route   anywhichway as long as it's West

Lift 1   Rosslare to Wexford

Meet another Mike on the boat who drives a converted bus with couch bed carpet (persian) cooker running water and a sound system with 200 cassettes   he plays Ian Dury all the way
there are bamboo paintings where the adverts used to be   in Morocco he ran someone down dead   it wasn't his fault but the police wanted money and he didn't have any   so pretending to be sick gasping for water   he stole back his passport and split

Lift 2   Wexford to Waterford

A nameless new car driven by a nameless semi-retired civil servant who interviews people   his name isn't important he talked non-stop about what he resents about TV radio newspapers and public important people who stir up issues where there is none "The Irish don't care one way or the other about contraception"   anyway I said in parting that this country seems underpopulated

Lift 3 Waterford to Cork

Rescued from a deluge by two workers in an electrical repair van   soaked to the skin   my legs dyed blue from my new bib and bracers   sitting on the floor in the back with tools and wires   we stop to do jobs along the way   pick up two Germans from Stuttgart   after pizzaland and black coffee in Cork   buy black rain trousers

Lift 4 Cork to Killarney Road

Short ride in a cash and carry truck from Cork centre to Killarney Road   he doesn't like driving but doesn't know what else to do

Lift 5 Killarney Road plus 10 miles

        Daniel Joseph Collins
        Long Valley Farm
        Newcestown 19
        Bandon Cork

a farmer with five children   his second youngest daughter a 21-year-old nurse has just had a nervous breakdown   and she had another breakdown 12 months ago   he talks   I listen   and think I understand   he invites me to come and stay on his farm anytime

Lift 6 Bandon plus another 10 miles

        walking
        quiet river
        flowing
        towards Cork

no rain wind rules the sky stopping I stand still and wait play my flute and wait until a surgeon in training at Cork General Hospital   drives a new car plays squash and football and does a bit of TM   so we talk about meditation   gives me his address and "look me up sometime" he says

Lift 7   to Killarney

after two hours   now a red lorry   a policeman doing a bit
of extra work on the side   "married and scalded" (with
children)
a good driver and a good drive 28 miles into Killarney
where I drink my first Guinness and remember

                the dead calf
                millions of maggots
                on the road
                to Killarney

                smell of lilac
                millions of flowers

Lift 8 Killarney to Kilmackerin West

Paddy a timber merchant going my way all the way to
Cahersiveen through the Balochoisin Pass with rain heavy and
no windshield wipers   steering bad   brakes bad   petrol
gauge doesn't work but we get there   Paddy patiently helps
me find Kilmackerin   a kind sensitive storyteller wanting
nothing in return but a promise not to tell anyone in case it
gets back to his firm   bidding farewell he says he's not
Paddy at all and doesn't work as a timber merchant and he's
on his way to Tralee Fayre.

Dance from Kilmackerin West

        walk
walking to the river
         cool breeze
cool breeze on the bog
         not much sun
         to dry the peat

                walking
                        to the river
                breeze
                        on the bog

why walk
        to the river

                      to the river

        why
        to see

                seeing
                        what is there

but you've been
                before
       you've been   *before*
so maybe
                maybe to smell
       smelling
                what wasn't there
before
       stop
                stopping
                      on the bog
stopping in the middle
                      by the peat

       sit   *sitting*
                    on a pile of peat
sitting on a pile of peat
       listen   *listening*
                    to the air
stand   *standing*
       turn   *turning*
       re turning
                        thoughts
walk   walking   *walking*
walking back to kilmackerin
       kilmackerin west

       image   *imaging*
imagining the river
       as it was
       as if it was

                empty   *empty*

a pretty girl

March morning birdsong & frogs mating
I stand by a silver loch flashing on the shore
waiting for a rainbow, yellow spots
in the shallows flood back memories
of a lark singing above the roar of white
water & light streaking across a leafless glen
with trees grating & squeaking, as clouds
part memories fade, a pretty girl pushes
her doll up the snowy hill, her purple
rucksack matches her purple dress

First teacher

Sechzig jahre alt. Erste reise nach Spanien, Fahrt durch Cezanne's Land.	Twenty years old, hitch hiking from Paris to Spain, June 67.
In der Nähe von Lyon biete ich einem jungen Mann an mitzufahren.	I get a lift from a German man who owns a laundry in
Er spricht Englisch und Französisch. Ich spreche Deutsch und Russisch	Düsseldorf. I speak English and French. He speaks German and Russian
Er hat einen Französisch / Spanisch Reiseführer. Ich einen Deutsch/Spanisch	He has a Spanish/ German phrase book. I have a Spanish/French
Reiseführer. Zwischen langen Pausen, versuchen wir's in Spanisch. Ich	phrase book – between long pauses we splutter in Spanish. He takes
nehme ihn den ganzen Weg bis zur Costa Brava mit.	me all the way to Costa Brava. We sleep that night on a
Für die Nacht halten wir am Strand . Er schläft für eine Weile.	beach. Well I sleep, he sits on a sand dune. I wake at 3 to piss.

Ich sitze die ganze nacht auf einer Düne. Er erwacht um 3 weil	He still sits staring at the sea. In the morning he's still up-
er muss. Zum Frühstück am Morgen fragt er mich in Spanisch:	right – alert – awake. At breakfast I ask in Spanish: ?*Algana*
?Algama vez duermes? Und ich antworte – No solumente me	*vez duermes?* And he said: *no solamente me siento.* Then
siento, dann erzähle Ich ihm von Yoga und Meditation	he told me about yoga and meditation and to be careful
und beim Üben von Pranayana Atmen aufzupassen.	when practising pran ayama breathing. He asked me for my
Zurück in Düsseldorf, schicke ich ihm drei Bücher über Mantra,	P.O. box in Spain. I forgot about him, till three months later
Hatha und Raja Yoga. Habe seitdem nichts von ihm gehört.	I received recorded delivery – three books all in English on
	raja, hatha and mantra yoga. I've practised ever since.
	Now I'm his age.

unspoken intimacy

After our long sleep in separate rooms
I salute my flatmate

who warms our shared toilet seat.
Her bum touches the same wood moments before mine.

In silence I pee and give thanks
for her unintended gift of body heat.

I salute my flatmate
for the gift of this morning's slow gradual awakening

after our long sleep in separate dreams.

"Things I Learned Last Week"*

A man from Palo Alto knows
how to smile for a camera.

My son only wants to be
with his girlfriend.

Pigs don't eat lemon and orange peel,
broccoli nor chocolate.

When Autumn Equinox and Jewish new year
       happen together
light and dark are in balance and I perform Tashlich
the ritual of tossing stale bread in a stream
while saying what I leave behind from last year.

The familiar language of pigs
is easy to understand.

Some of us believe
that to leave a toilet seat up
when not in use will drain energy
and lose you money.

* *title of a poem by William Stafford*

Notes

Butterfly Bones: this is the **sphenoid bone** (from Greek *sphenoeides*, "wedgelike") situated at the base of the skull in front of the temporals and basilar part of the occipital bone. The sphenoid bone somewhat resembles a butterfly or bat with its wings extended, and it lies in the transverse plane. The **Sphenoid** is one of the more difficult bones to describe. It is the only bone that goes horizontally through the skull, making a base for the brain and a ceiling for the mouth. It also supports the pituitary gland and is one of the seven bones forming the socket of the eye. My friend Janet had a malignant tumour near her pituitary gland, pressing on her sphenoid bone. This poem was written for her and read to her before she died. She flew.

Hindrance: traditionally there are five recognizable hindrances (distractions) to concentration (in meditation), and everyone experiences all of them some of the time. The five hindrances are: (1) desire for sensory experience, (2) ill-will, (3) restlessness and anxiety, (4) sloth and torpor, (5) doubt and indecision. The 'ill-will' in this poem came from a disturbing experience that kept coming to mind for months and years after the event, especially when I meditated – I would hear her voice justifying what she did... Since writing the poem, she has been quiet.

57 All Saints Road: is where David Hart lives, the 1997–98 Birmingham poet laureate. He has been a pioneer in promoting the arts in health, and his prize-winning poetry is an inspiration to me.

Carbeth changes: Carbeth is twenty minutes by bus from Glasgow – a scattering of small huts in the hills along the West Highland Way by a lochan. Most Wednesdays I go to a friend's hut to write.

Poetry from Two Ravens Press

Castings: by Mandy Haggith
£8.99. ISBN 978-1-906120-01-6. Published February 2007

Leaving the Nest: by Dorothy Baird
£8.99. ISBN 978-1-906120-06-1. Published July 2007

The Zig Zag Woman: by Maggie Sawkins
£8.99. ISBN 978-1-906120-08-5. Published September 2007

In a Room Darkened: by Kevin Williamson
£8.99. ISBN 978-1-906120-07-8. Published October 2007

Running with a Snow Leopard: by Pamela Beasant
£8.99. ISBN 978-1-906120-14-6. Published January 2008

In the Hanging Valley: by Yvonne Gray
£8.99. ISBN 978-1-906120-19-1. Published March 2008

The Atlantic Forest: by George Gunn
£8.99. ISBN 978-1-906120-26-9. Published April 2008

For more information on these and other titles, and for extracts and author interviews, see our website.

Titles are available direct from the publisher at
www.tworavenspress.com
or from any good bookshop.